T0314754

STELLA

Neil Bartlett

STELLA

OBERON BOOKS
LONDON

WWW.OBERONBOOKS.COM

Introduction

HISTORY (1); 'WOULDN'T IT BE DREADFUL,
IF THIS WAS A TRUE STORY?'

Well, it is. This play-script is, amongst other things, a love letter sent to a very real person. It is not a literal account of the life and death in question, but it *is* closely inspired by an (incredible) set of truths.

The real Stella – Ernest Boulton – was born to respectable lower-middle-class parents in the London suburb of Tottenham, in 1848. In 1868, after failing to make a success of working as a bank clerk, Ernest Boulton was still living at home – at 23 Shirland Road, Maida Vale – but as well cultivating an extravagantly effeminate male look and manner in his daily life was also living large parts of that life under the female alias of Stella Clinton. Stella Clinton was a lady – a member of polite society, with her own engraved calling-cards, a wedding ring, a private hairdresser, a cultivated taste for the respectable amateur and professional theatrical performances in which she performed exclusively female roles – and a flat on Southampton Street, just off the Strand. However, Stella also had another side; sometimes Ernest changed his clothes – and identity – at a much less salubrious address, in rented premises on Wakefield Street (just south of St Pancras) and then went out on the town with a select group of fellow queens masquerading as a very different kind of lady. This Stella was an extravagantly gowned and highly conspicuous sex-worker. The current evidence suggests that Stella could, when she chose, pass as a woman in both of these identities. It also suggests that she delighted in taking the risks that are inevitably involved in choosing to alter who you say (and possibly feel) you are as often as you change your clothes.

Remarkably, Ernest's mother seems to have approved of this dangerous lifestyle, or at least of those parts of it that she knew about. Mrs Boulton may have been influenced in her apparent broad-mindedness by the fact that by 1869 her son's current lover was an extremely financially generous (if sadly unattractive) minor aristocrat and Tory MP, one Lord Arthur Pelham-Clinton. It was Arthur who showered Stella with presents on her twenty-first birthday, Arthur who had given Stella the wedding ring she wore in her more respectable persona, and Arthur who paid for the West End flat where the two of them slept together as man and wife.

In 1870, shortly after that twenty-first birthday, Stella was arrested on the pavement of the Aldwych in London and charged with conspiracy to commit a felony after she and an equally cross-dressed friend had repaired to the ladies toilet of the now-demolished Royal Strand Theatre in order to adjust their drag. They had been seen making sexual advances to male members of the audience; the felony in question was, therefore, sodomy. The police records do not indicate if Stella was wearing Arthur's wedding ring to go with the flaming silk evening gown she was wearing that night, but we do know that Arthur wasn't there – Stella was out on the town with her best friend Fanny (aka one Mr. Frederick Park) and a couple of pieces of straight trade who they had picked up together earlier in the evening. The two of them were then sensationally tried in a widely discussed and reported trial – and equally sensationally acquitted, for lack of material evidence of the specific anatomical act in question.

Conventional wisdom dictates that anyone branded a homosexual in Victorian London – and especially anyone who had appeared on the front pages of most of the popular London newspapers as an effeminate and dubiously-behaved cross-dresser – would be obliged to disappear. Not a bit of it. Ernest Boulton changed his name (to Ernest Byne), dyed his hair blond and went on tour as a professional drag act – and then left the country and reappeared in New York, working as a top-billed female impersonator in a series of minor theatres on the fringes of Broadway. This work gradually dried up as he lost his sensational good looks; he changed his name again, this time to Ernest Blair, and returned to Britain in 1877 to tour for another gruelling twenty-five years on the lower end of the British provincial variety circuit, relying on his wardrobe, the remains of his once-lovely soprano voice and his outrageous press clippings from nearly thirty years before to get him his bookings. He seems to have performed his signature tune, a sentimental parlour-ballad entitled 'Fading Away', at almost all of these engagements. One of Stella's last known addresses was on Euston Street, in Somerstown, London – just round the back of Euston Station – which indicates straightened circumstances at the end of his life. He died from a brain tumour in London in 1904, in the National Hospital, Queen Square, Holborn – and therefore presumably dressed as a man. He was fifty-six.

Arthur's name was immediately connected with Stella's after her arrest. Shortly afterwards, his sudden death in a provincial hotel-room was reported in *The Times* – a couple of days after he had been issued with a subpoena to appear as a witness at her trial. If his death was in fact suicide, which seems the most likely possibility, we now know no more about exactly where, how or why Arthur killed himself than Stella herself most probably ever did. We currently have no evidence that she ever saw or heard from him again after she was arrested.

HISTORY (2)

Please remember that this text is the script for a piece of theatre. If you want to know more of the actual facts, there is a fuller account of Stella's arrest and trial in my 1988 book *Who Was That Man?* – and Stella, along with her partner in crime Fanny, is all over the internet these days, with many pictures of her in both her London and New York heydays available online, and quite a body of recent popular and academic writing about her available in all good bookshops. Although I (almost) agree with Oscar Wilde that to be suggestive for fiction is to be of more importance than a fact, I would not want anything I've written here to assume the status of evidence – for instance, such details as my moving of the date of Arthur's death from June 15th to a wintry January 15th, or my moving of Stella's fatal cancer from her brain to the beautiful and famously talented throat with which she had earned at least two of her livings. These details were dictated by internal patterns of imagery, not by history.

I make no apology for the fact that this play presents Stella on her own, whereas she is now almost invariably only ever talked of as being one half of a double act – 'Fanny and Stella'. The writing of this piece began with the image of a middle-aged man in a suit, alone in a darkened room, completely silent and under a nameless threat. It was only after a considerable period of work that this image attached itself to the story of Ernest Boulton, a figure who I thought I'd already dealt with in my work of nearly thirty years earlier. Perhaps it was the loneliness of the end of his life that made him come back into my mind. That, and his courage. The two things are not unconnected.

HISTORY (3); ERNEST/STELLA

Since she lived in the years before hormones and gender re-assignment, we have no way of knowing if Ernest/Stella sounded like or identified herself as what we would now call a trans woman as well as – or sometimes perhaps instead of – what we would now call a drag queen or a female impersonator or just a plain old homosexual. The play does not argue the toss one way or another – Stella's final incarnation as a fifty-six-year-old man, for instance, seems to me something that she would have experienced as being as real as the drag and passing identities of her younger life.

On the subject of gender-fluidity, I would like to thank my friends and colleagues Justin V Bond, Jo Clifford, Ivan Cartwright, Bette Bourne, Scottee, Elliot and Greygorey for talking to me at such length while I was writing the play, and telling me (from their radically different, distinctive and very personal perspectives) what it has felt like for each of them to become, impersonate or work as a person of a physical gender different to the one they were born in, and to acknowledge that many of the things which they told me have found their way directly into my Stella's mouth, mixed with such fragments of her nineteenth-century voice as have survived in her letters, reviews, police-records and playscripts. I would like to most especially thank the great *onnagata* Nakamura Tokizo V for his generosity in sharing with me some of his experience of inhabiting female roles in the Japanese kabuki theatre. I have worked with drag queens all my life, but seeing and hearing the mystery of transformation treated with the extraordinary depth and respect which Tokizo-san brings to his art opened my eyes to new ways of thinking about it when I met him in Nagoya in 2014. He was also the person who pointed out the possible significance of the fact that Stella was my current age when she died, and who first asked me Stella's question about whether it is possible to die as anyone except oneself.

While we're giving credit where credit is due, I would also like to thank the young man who threatened to kill me while I was crossing Leicester Square one fine spring evening in 1986, just because I was wearing three-inch heels and a little black dress. He is also doubtless one of the reasons why I wrote this piece.

THIS SCRIPT.

As so often with my work, this is far from being a conventional script – the images and the occasion are as important as the words. If you are reading the piece without ever having seen it, I'd like to share the following, in order to give you at least some sense of how it might all work.

This is as much an encounter as a performance – an encounter with a very special person. There is a gaunt-faced, middle-aged man, in a suit, sitting in the dark, waiting. He starts to talk. But who is he talking *to*? It turns out that this man has spent most of his life in the theatre, but now finds himself profoundly alone, in a shabby room, on a shabby street, very close to the end of his life. It is quite possible that talking out loud to an imaginary audience is quite natural to him – especially on this strange and potentially final morning of his life. He is also, as it turns out, heavily drugged.

Then, from nowhere, and for no good reason, a second man appears – young, glittering, sexy, infuriating – dressing for a party, but as yet mostly undressed – laughing and pouting through a cloud of face-powder and tatty innuendo.

The older man says he is waiting for a cab to arrive at seven in the morning; this second, younger man says he is also waiting for a cab to arrive, but at seven in the evening. This cab is coming to take him to what he hopes will be an especially glamorous and significant party, thrown for him by his lover. The older man's cab seems to have been ordered to take him somewhere of a very different significance.

Quite soon, I think, the audience will begin to realise that these two people are the same person – that what I have written is in fact a one-man show for two bodies. A single life is being scrutinised from two very different perspectives; one of them is trying to finds the courage to end something, and the other is trying to find the courage to start. Both, as it turns out, are terrified.

We all know that it is impossible, even in a crisis, either to travel back in time to advise our younger selves or to travel into the future to ask our future selves for advice. Audiences must decide for themselves whether this impossibility is in fact tampered with in the final pages of my play. Stranger things have happened.

One last thing. All the time I was writing, a third figure kept materialising in my imagination – one who isn't even mentioned in the script. He seemed to be emphatically male, and entered my imagination in a black coat and a hat, as if he had come from outside – whereas both of my Stellas are very definitely inside, waiting for knocks on their respective doors. Sometimes I thought of this third figure as The Ferryman – the one who has come to take Stella on her last journey – and sometimes, more mundanely, as simply The Cabdriver. In rehearsals, he began to acquire some of the prop-handling functions of a *kuroko* or stage-assistant from the Japanese kabuki. He also began to suggest a shadow of the absent lovers who haunt the play. For want of a better name, we finally christened him The Attendant. His presence is not obligatory in any future production. Or it could be multiplied.

The playing time should be about seventy minutes. No set whatsoever is necessary, or even any evocation of an exact period, because this play takes place somewhere where nothing much matters any more except the body itself.

I very much hope you enjoy meeting Stella.

Neil Bartlett, May 2016.

Stella was originally created by the following company;

Performers

ONE	Richard Cant
TWO	Oscar Batterham
THREE	David Carr

Text and Direction	Neil Bartlett
Design	Rae Smith
Lights	Rick Fisher with Martin McLachlan
Sound	Christopher Shutt, with Dinah Mullen
Costumes	Johanna Coe
Music	Nicolas Bloomfield
Vocal Coach	Rebecca Root
Make-up	Francois Testory

Producer	Polly Thomas
Casting	Siobhan Bracke
Stage and Company Manager	Leona Nally

Stella was co-commissioned by the Brighton Festival, the London International Festival of Theatre and the Holland Festival. The first performance was at the Theatre Royal Brighton on 27 May 2016.

Neil Bartlett would like to thank Gary Carter, Shojiku Productions, LIFT, the Amsterdam Festival and Alison Duthie at the King's Cultural Institute for supporting the research that lead towards the decision to write this piece; Paul Griffiths, Ronald Cavaye, Tetsuo Yanai, Tim Clark and Mark Okira for their help before, during and after his time in Tokyo and Nagoya as he immersed himself in the world of the kabuki and tried to think again about theatre and how it could tell this story; Ruth Mckenzie, Mark Ball and Andrew Comben for their personal as well as their professional support; Fay Davies for her encouragement; the staff of the British and Wellcome Libraries for helping him track down Ernest Boulton's original playscripts in the Lord Chamberlain's Collection and accurate records of what throat-cancer surgery was like in 1904 respectively.

This script is respectfully dedicated to Nakamura Tokizo V, with his kind permission.

Please note; The stage directions refer to both ONE and TWO as both 'he' and 'she' – as is common in Queer English. In the original production both parts were played by cis-gendered male actors, but I see no reason why this story could not be told by actors of either gender, or neither.

ONE, discovered.

Fifty-six.

It is early morning.

A chair; a bag; a glass.

He has a bloody handkerchief wrapped around the knuckles of his right hand.

ONE   When? When was the last time?

Years ago.

Three, almost exactly. Or was it four?

As if it matters.

A silence.

As if it matters which century all this
happened in.

A silence.

Where? Where, now?

A gesture.

As you see; a modest but reasonably
furnished front sitting-room....

Dark, still.

Practical doorway up right, a black horsehair
ottoman of the cheaper sort downstage
centre; no mirrors at all.....

A silence.

One large mirror, over the fireplace, but
covered. For some reason. One small bag,
packed and ready.

A silence.

Why?

Why am I talking out loud, you mean?
Because –

She takes a sip from a glass of water.

– Thank you – because I would like to stop
thinking; because I always thought I was

good at waiting, but apparently, in the event,
I'm not;

A silence.

Because there's no one else here.

Will that do? Will that do, as an explanation.

Or possibly even a reason....

Another sip.

Because the cab will be here at seven, and
it is now not quite a quarter of six, and
therefore

Panic; quelled.

Therefore it is still rather early.

A silence.

How Does One Pass The Time; *that* is the
question...

She rummages through papers in her bag. She extracts a letter.

> *My dear*
>
> *All those who declare that everything in England
> has changed, well what would they say to a
> snowfall such as this? Deep enough to bury a lover
> on a country road. Deep enough to bury a lover on
> a country road exclamation. Really, a winter such
> as we last knew in our childhoods. Speaking of
> lovers, I write to tell you*

A silence.

And so on.

She turns the letter over

> *...It has been a wonder knowing you, but all
> good things etc. Do take care, and I shall certainly*

*forward an address as soon as I have one. Goodbye
is a dreadful word, so I shan't write it, but merely
wish you all the best with your*

*With your adventures, of which there surely will
be many.*

Devotedly, yours

She puts it back in the bag.

Though in what possible sense he was ever
that.

In what sense they were ever, any of them,
that.

A silence.

Actually would you excuse me –

She takes a sip of water.

I mustn't miss it, you see. The knock. On the
door.

I do apologise if anyone feels I've falsely
raised their expectations.

Of confidences being exchanged.

Silence.

She tidies herself and puts the bag on the floor.

Silence. A gesture.

There!

A burst of laughter and applause. Quietly;

Thank you.

Silence. She changes her mind.

I'm sorry....

She repeats her opening gesture, and tries her opening lines again with a slightly different emphasis.

> As you see; a darkened room, a door upstage right.

> The mirror over the fireplace seems to have been broken, but by whom or why is not yet clear. Glass everywhere....

She touches the handkerchief. Silence

> Please try not to worry – I'm sure she still has sufficient time to say whatever it is she needs to say.

Silence.

> Although it must be a quarter of, now, at least. Don't you think?

Silence.

> Or even ten minutes of. Or even five.

TWO.

Twenty-one – just. Nearly naked. Bright hair…

Early evening.

Entering;

TWO	'Just a minute!'

Laughter and applause.

It never does mean that, does it?

Using a hand-mirror, he begins to work on his face.

Honestly – Time – people do make such a fuss. Time….Not to mention Decisions…

Cerise Silk, tonight. Brand-new from the box. Mother – who lord knows has never made a wise decision in her life – always says Choosing is the Paramount Art. Presenting Oneself In The Best Light, she calls it… though personally I think Being Sufficiently Obvious might be a better turn of phrase. Life is, after all – let's be frank – best understood as a Display Window. These days.

Actually I've got plenty. Seven o'clock, Arthur said, for the cab.

I do hope it's a better place than last week's. Last week's was dreary in the extreme – honestly, barely enough people to raise a titter, never mind a round. I made him make up for it later – made him stay downstairs for hours – although I'm not quite sure he understood. Obviously I'm not expecting bouquets from *complete* strangers when I make my entrance, but I'm hardly going to all this trouble to be *not* stared at of an evening, am I? Especially not tonight. If I wanted that sort of treatment, I could just

A silence.

Well I could just stay at Home.

Or Prison, as I like to call it. The Mirrors aren't big enough, the Questions are never the right ones and all Approval is qualified.

Hence, Arthur.

No, he isn't handsome, not even remotely. Since you ask. Short, sweaty – thinning, on top, already, which is revolting at his age… And he's clumsy – tears things, all the time. But…Since the Gentleman is Rich… as Mama always puts it….he is able to provide me with exactly what I need. At this point in my career.

Apparently the lampshades in this new place are the most flattering in London.

People do say, of course

They say the way you're carrying on it's only a matter of the aforementioned

You know

Time.

A silence.

Before there's trouble, they mean.

Mama, in particular, means.

A silence.

Well, if it happens –

Trouble –

If it happens, mind –

Arthur's got his money,and I've got my answers. All right ready and folded neatly in my bag.

A pantomime;

> Certainly not, officer! Do I look as if I'm in that line of work ?
>
> Please don't touch me.
>
> Well why don't you ask the gentleman; he's the one taking me home. To an apartment he rents specifically for that purpose. Would you like me to write down the address for you, it's in rather a good part of town.
>
> Why thank you officer. And Goodnight to you too.

The work on his face resumes.

> Of course, it would be lovely to have a crystal ball – or, a Playbill – you know, of one's own life – Scene One A Rustic Glade, Scene Two – barely a year later – The Fairy Castle, with all its glorious furnishings – that kind of thing – so that you'd always know, you know, what to expect... but who are you going to get to set *me* up in type eh? Always a question, and never an answer, me. A glimpse, but never a guaranteed breakfast. A sip, a slip, a wink and a wriggle. Always.
>
> Except with Arthur. Possibly. We'll see.

He surveys his handiwork so far in the mirror.

> Skin like a girl. Like a girl on her summer holidays.
>
> Rosy all over.
>
> Yes including down below.

He starts work again.

I think most people have no idea............I
mean no idea how much work this all is...
and that's just my Outsides!..A friend of mine
says you just have to want absolutely nothing
else in life, and I think she's right really;
Absolute Dedication – that's the trick...that,
and a little bit of red under the black of the
eyebrow...there, there's the evening's first bit
of free good advice for you – and this early
in the proceedings too. Well it never hurts to
suggest the blood beneath the skin, does it?
– as that friend of mine I mentioned always
says...And she should know.

Item, two true-blue eyes...

Item two lips; Indifferent; Red....

Do excuse me – Arthur said seven prompt
for the cab, and this can take ages. Honestly.
Now...

He begins work on his mouth...

ONE   Oh why now, honestly. Why now, after all
                    these years.

He adjusts the handkerchief on his knuckles.

                    At a quarter of six in the morning.

He takes out the letter again.

                    *… speaking of lovers, I write to tell you, in case
                    you haven't heard out there on the road, that the
                    papers down here are reporting the death of your
                    one and only as was. I'm sorry if this is the first
                    you've heard – being the bearer etc was never my
                    favourite role – and will leave all the details to the
                    clipping enclosed.*

He looks at the clipping.

A silence.

                    I remember asking the boy who delivered it
                    how on earth they planned to get the body
                    into the ground.

*TWO **has smudged his lip.***

TWO   Oh how awful....

ONE   Frozen, you see.

TWO   Horrible.

ONE   Iron.

TWO   Really horrible....

ONE   That particular winter. The fifteenth?

He looks at the clipping again.

                    Of January. I thought so.....

The fault on the lip has been corrected.

TWO   There!!

ONE	People never talk about a verdict of *Life* by Misadventure, do they. Why is that, do you think?

A pantomime of girlishness. To start with at least...

TWO	– Well thank you very much. Yes I am pretty – some would say the prettiest of them all, in this colour. Yes my gown was a present actually, and from somebody rather special. Why tonight, you silly. Twenty-one. Why thank you. No you can't! Well perhaps later you can. Alright, definitely later.
	Later, you can kiss me. You can kiss me, and then, you can marry me. Whenever and however you want. I'm very good at it you know. Especially when no one's watching.
	Yes I do like that.
ONE	As an infant, she dazzled.
TWO	Go on then;
ONE	Father abhorred her, Mother adored her and they'd moved seven times by the time she was eight.
TWO	Lick the envelope, why don't you. Lick it and stick it.......lick the stamp too while you're down there.
ONE	School was a disgrace.
TWO	Yes, I'll tell you when to stop...
ONE	At eighteen, her feet barely touched the ground; doors were opened – there were jewels – and the first articles about her appeared as a matter of course. Her throat especially received acclaim. Such noises!!!
TWO	Sssh! – here comes Arthur...

ONE	Such pantomimes; such makings-do!!
TWO	Arthur approaching –
ONE	There were hands everywhere, of course –
TWO	Arthur across the room –
ONE	Doormen –
TWO	Arthur smiling –
ONE	Ushers –
TWO	Arthur with a ring –
ONE	Waiters,
TWO	In a box –
ONE	Shop-men,
TWO	In his pocket –
ONE	Cabbies;
TWO	For me –
ONE	Gloved –
TWO	For later.
ONE	Ungloved…
TWO	For ever! Possibly.
ONE	She wore out names like evening shoes; alibis – torn and rendered useless. Miss Adventure, Miss Leading; Miss Giving, Miss Spent. Miss Used.
TWO	Well you never know.
ONE	Miss Taken. Miss Taken – because when it finally happened, –
TWO	I mean, it *is* my birthday.

ONE	– when the arresting hand finally descended on her well-shaped shoulder – and she found herself in the papers for all the *wrong* reasons
TWO	We'll see…
ONE	She was, of all things, surprised.
TWO	I said; we'll *see.*

A silence.

ONE	Surprised. On that very particular evening.
	Still…you haven't really lived until you've been well and truly fucked, as she always used to say.
	Until you've tasted that particular brand of well-aimed spittle. 'Til you've been *judged.*
TWO	Now, speaking *of* jewellery….

He selects a small fitted jewel-case.

ONE	The day after the verdict
	The day after

She cannot continue.

	Now do excuse me –
TWO	Happiness, in a box. Well – as Mama says – how else did you think it comes?

ONE extracts a small medicine bottle from her bag, and adds three drops of an opiate painkiller to her glass of water.

She sips.

TWO opens the box, which contains earrings. He puts them on, and looks in his mirror.

TWO   Ah…

ONE   Ah! They said I shouldn't, really. Talk. Out loud. It exacerbates the *condition,* apparently. But under the circumstances.

               Thank you. Ah! Better.

She clears her throat, waiting for the morphine to numb it a little. TWO opens another box of earrings.

TWO   Yes – better…

ONE   Where was I? Where? Oh yes. The day after. Thank you.

               The day after the verdict – the day after she had been discussed, branded and abandoned – she thought she might visit the zoo. Visit the zoo, choose a seat in front of some cages and try and work out which stinking or shrieking beast in particular people thought she had now overnight become. Gibbon, or cat? Or perhaps, she thought, the opera, to see if that was an even better place to scream out loud without anyone realising it was actually you making all that frightening noise. She quite lost the power of speech, I remember, for several hours, and had to borrow a stub of pencil from a publican on the Euston Road in order to write down the words which had been running round her head ever since the judge had pronounced, namely; *Wouldn't it be dreadful if this was actually happening.*

               Wouldn't it be dreadful, if this was all a true story.

Imagine.

In fact, once it was dark again and the panic had subsided

As it always does

In my experience

Eventually

She walked home, went upstairs and packed. She knew she'd never hear from him again, you see, knew it at once – even though the judge had said there was insufficient material evidence of that particular misdemeanor, had said she *wasn't guilty…* Which was a joke, when you think of what she had been wearing that night and why. When you recall what she was really thinking about. If you know what I mean. If you were ever there.

Why thank you, I will.

She takes the glass again.

He never wrote, even. Never. Nothing – I heard Nothing, until that letter.

She sips.

But…; but. But I

She.

But, she didn't disappear.

She Toured….Made Disgrace her Profession, Confession, her Forte; Catastrophe, her stock in trade. Well can one be surprised? Under the circumstances, the stage doubtless seemed – of all the things it is most decidedly not – a Natural choice. I remember her telling me once, over tea – no, please, useless

to recall any particular boarding-house
names after all this time – remember her
telling me that even years afterwards she
often found herself wishing she'd had that
verdict embroidered into the linings of some
of her subsequent costumes. Shepherdess,
Governess, Reckless, Loveless – you
know, all the minor yet rewarding roles.
'Not Guilty' – she found it hard, she said,
sometimes, to remember that those had
been the judge's actual words – felt the need,
she said, sometimes, of some reminder,
some delicate yet pointed reminder of the
neccessity of constantly aspiring to that
elusive yet reputedly marvellous condition of
human existence, that magical condition of
being *not guilty*.

Thirty.

She toured for thirty years – from when she
was twenty-one, until… Well as you see.

Trains, beds, locks, compromises – the
Atlantic ocean, twice, if you can believe
it, which you should. Packing, unpacking;
packing….honestly I could go on but she –
eventually – couldn't.

A sip of from the glass.

Thank you – Eventually – well, why dwell on
the details –

*Having changed his mind several times over the earrings, TWO
lifts a necklace from another fitted case.*

TWO   What d'you think?

Another sip.

ONE	Not that there wasn't laughter – because there was – at times –
TWO	They match, you see. Make a set.
ONE	and management were very kind in the end;
TWO	A pair…
ONE	nothing was said to her *face*,
TWO	A *couple*.
ONE	but it was made clear that no further bookings would be forthcoming on account of that particular asset.

*TWO **imagines an engagement ring on her finger.***

TWO	Oh Arthur! –
ONE	She accepted the moment –
TWO	For me? –
ONE	I won't say graciously,
TWO	Really?
ONE	but accept it she did.
TWO	Oh you shouldn't have…
ONE	After all,
TWO	Mama!!
ONE	no one wants to end their career overhearing some young man in a saloon bar saying to his friend well I thought it was actually rather interesting to see the part played by someone who has lost their looks entirely. She had a dread of that. A horror.

Curiously, she sang until the very end.

Then,

TWO	Yes Mama, yes I am…
ONE	She packed, and unpacked – seeking ever, well, frankly cheaper accommodation,until… Well shall we simply say *the slope steepened* and leave it at that? It steepened, until she found herself

She repeats her very first gesture again.

As you see.

I do apologise about the mirror. Glass on the floor hardly shows a room to best advantage, does it – really, somebody could cut themselves. It's an odd sensation, smashing one's own face, but trust me, one determined fist and the whole thing simply gives way. The sound is not unlike that of a bone breaking. Or a footstep in deep snow.

Remember to take your rings off, would be my advice.

Should you have any left.

An edge of hysteria.

You see that was always the first thing you made sure of – always, as soon as you arrived; never mind a window; *was there a mirror, in the dressing room.* Had sufficient provision been made for checking that you were exactly who you'd told them you were going to be that particular evening. Told him, whoever he was, who you were going to be. Later.

Can you imagine.

Can you imagine, exclamation.

For thirty years.

TWO	Happy Birthday to me.
ONE	I keep on thinking there is something I haven't said, you see. Or done.

She picks up and clutches the bag that contains the letter.

TWO	'Happy Birthday to me…'
ONE	Said – do excuse me will you but I do need to be *ready. Ready.*

ONE starts warming up her voice as if for a performance. TWO tries out her freshly painted lips in her mirror.

TWO	'Happy Birthday to….me!'

Laughter and Applause.

'Happy birthday, dear……'

It's all a question of being prepared, isn't it? In Life as in Art….

ONE	**A-a-aaah!**
TWO	And why assume things'll be a disaster? They might be rather fun. You never know.
ONE	**Ah! Ah! Ah!**
TWO	And what's the odds, so long as you're happy? I mean you're not twenty-one for the rest of your life, are you?
ONE	**Ah. Aaaah.**
TWO	Oh the horror.

TWO looks in her mirror, loving what she sees. ONE begins to stretch her throat in a scream. Almost no sound comes out.

ONE	**AAAAAAAh!! AAAAh!!**
TWO	The horror!
ONE	**Help me!**

TWO	Too soon to dress, I'm afraid. We mustn't crumple – not before he gets here, anyway......
ONE	**Somebody help me.**
TWO	La la la. Exciting!
ONE	**Please. I'm not finished.**
TWO	Lampshades; Cerise... Lovely!
ONE	**I'm not finished. I'm not finished.**

*TWO **looks at his imaginary ring again and giggles, as***

KNOCKING

LAUGHTER AND APPLAUSE.

THEY BOTH HEAR THE KNOCKING.

DARKNESS.

LIGHTS UP.

The same, a few moments later.

ONE facing upstage; TWO holding a torn-open envelope and a letter.

ONE   'Not coming, will write later.'

                 Later; as in half an hour later, do you think,
                 or as in start without me and pay your own
                 fucking cab into town for a change? Later as
                 in temporary hitch, or later as in no plans for
                 moving things onto a more formal footing
                 on the occasion of your birthday whatsoever,
                 actually. No plans for a ring, for instance, not
                 tonight or any other.

                 Honestly.

He reads the letter again.

                 'Not coming' – 'Not coming' – which rather
                 begs the question of who I am doing all this
                 for, don't you think?

A silence. ONE turns.

ONE   It was next door.

TWO   I have a horror of doing it for myself, you
                 see. If there aren't any faces around to reflect
                 me, then I do tend

ONE   Asking if I needed anything carrying.

TWO   I panic.

ONE   – I explained that under the circumstances
                 No, but kind anyway.

TWO   I said I panic, alright?

ONE   Do excuse me, I feel suddenly rather

ONE sits down, shaken – seeing the street outside has shown him how much closer it now is to seven a.m. than he would like it to be.

TWO   *(A pantomime, using his hand-mirror as a prop.)*

You see when Papa stares I am one thing;
when Mama, another. In the hallway,
another; with the cabbie, another; when
the first heads turn as I step down onto
the pavement another; when a gentleman
in the row behind leans forward to check,
another; when his friend – who's only come
for a gander, you understand, to see what
one looks like in the actual *flesh* – also leans
forward, and smiles and says excuse me
but –which Arthur always hates by the way,
really hates – well that makes a fifth or sixth
thing and it's still not even supper-time – and
of course all that makes me laugh, it can
make me laugh for hours on dizzy end when
I'm in the mood, but when there's suddenly
nobody, when suddenly there's only *this* for
your friend of an evening, well – well it does
leave you not knowing whether you're all of
those people simultaneously or none of them
at all, and quite frankly it's bewildering. It
makes me feel

It makes me feel, sometimes, as if I'm
running through some great, locked *house*,
with no protection or company whatsoever,
not a shred, and the thing is, there's no
furniture. No clue, anywhere. Just doors.
Empty. Doors.

This one happens quite often actually.

And in every room, you see, when I'm there,
there's a fireplace. Like a… mouth. As if
somebody was screaming but there's nothing

coming out. Somebody screaming but
making no noise whatsoever.

Oh me and my dreams! Mama says I take
too much coffee after dinner and that that
explains everything, but

ONE has picked up his bag and rested it in his lap.

ONE	Half past six at least, I should say, now. From the look of the light.
TWO	But I know it's not that –
ONE	It's just the one bag you're allowed, you see, because they don't want anybody thinking of the ward as their home – of planning a long stay or anything like that. Which is why I've nothing much from the carrying point of view. As I explained.
TWO	It's not that at all.
ONE	Indeed I might just take my purse, as I'll really only be needing my cab-fare.
TWO	No.
ONE	My cab-fare to the Hospital, but not back. Well we might as well be frank.
TWO	I just need

A silence.

ONE　　　　　Under the circumstances.

A silence.

I don't *think* she heard me screaming.

ONE retches and then vomits with fear. TWO speaks over her.

TWO　　　　　– I just need to be loved. Well is it too much
　　　　　　　　to ask, with my looks? And on my birthday.

Honestly I really thought tonight was the night – the cab, the dress, the lampshades,the ring, everything. Everything. Honestly.

He turns. Or leaves.

APPLAUSE

SILENCE

ONE finishes vomiting. The vomit has burnt her throat.

Do excuse me. Quite reminds me of that time at the Fulton Street Olympic. There she was, fourth billing, – fourth billing exclamation, you might say, but honestly she had rarely been gladder of the work, under the circumstances – anyway, as I say, there she was, Olympic, overture and beginners, same as always, one last smooth of the gown before you're on – and then the minute the music hit her she suddenly felt adrift, suddenly not quite herself, hardly Olympic at all if truth be told, quite

well quite untethered

and turning into the wing behind her for some advice or sustenance, some anything, actually, from anybody, answer came there none. Unsurprisingly, as she had been essentially working solo for years by that point, Olympic or otherwise – but that dark moment there on Fulton Street was I suppose in its way a pointer, a beginning one might say, a hint of things to come. Overture and beginners hardly covers it at all, actually, as a sensation. One feels. Crawling. All over.

So she really should have known.

As we all, really, should know. That the news is never good in the end.

TWO returns with a facecloth or napkin. ONE starts to clean himself as best he can with the bloody handkerchief from around his hand.

Do excuse me.

TWO   Sorry about that.

ONE   Terror is never convenient, is it?

TWO   But honestly.

ONE   And so rarely attractive.

TWO sets to work angrily removing her face.

Silence.

Do you know I don't think I have ever counted the minutes so intently, not even in an overture.

She pulls the letter with the clipping from her bag again.

January the 15ᵗʰ; Family only. No flowers.

TWO   Honestly, all this…planning….All this bloody *trouble*…

ONE   *Family… Only.*

TWO   And over who – Arthur? What's Arthur to me or me to Arthur that I should weep for him?

ONE   Quite. The boy was in a uniform. Marine blue serge, I think – if it matters….

TWO   Absolute nonsense, if I'm honest –

ONE   It must be such a relief, he said –

TWO	Absolute bollocks, the whole fucking pantomime.
ONE	Such a relief finally knowing what'd happened to him….
TWO	He knows, and I know,
ONE	But I didn't, you see –
TWO	Know that this isn't *it*,
ONE	I didn't know what had happened to him.
TWO	It's just the best either of us can manage.
ONE	Was it dark, the room?
TWO	Under the circumstances.
ONE	The room where he did it. Did he undress before making the first cut? Was there a mirror over the fireplace? You see despite the fact that several months had passed before I got this I still barely even knew *that* he'd gone, never mind *how* –
TWO	Mama must say what she likes, I shall break it off entirely –
ONE	Though in what sense they are ever, any of them, gone.
TWO	– and that Cerise Silk can go right back where it came from.
ONE	Any of them.
TWO	Well you never do know I must say.
ONE	If there's a mirror in the cubicle where they make you undress at the hospital I shall smash that too. Wrap a towel round my hand this time, and smash it. No man over fifty disrobes to advantage in my opinion.

A silence. TWO stares, but not into his mirror.

ONE has his hand at his throat.

> They call it the crab – did you know that? *Kanceros* – from the Greek. Cancer. Claws? I said, Oh yes doctor, that's exactly what you feel – pinching, just here…Clutching. Usually between four and five in the morning, when you really are underneath, really are beneath waves. 'Of course,' he said – the doctor, not the boy – 'it is bad news, but we shan't know what the true situation is until I'm actually right inside you.' Which sounded familiar. He said 'These anaesthetics have opened up a whole new country inside. A whole new country for us to explore. Inside.'
>
> He had hands like Arthur's – just like… Clean.

TWO resumes his cleaning. Furious.

TWO	And it's not as if he's a catch. Small hands; short – balding already, as I said, so you have to remember not to look down while he's on the job, which I hate; sweats –
ONE	Then he explained.
TWO	Tears things down below.
ONE	The room will be darkened;
TWO	And then apologises for doing it, which I really mind, because I do think a man should have the courage of his convictions in that department at least –
ONE	My head will be pushed back;
TWO	The sort of man I deserve, anyway.
ONE	And then there'll be the insertion.

TWO	A darkened room –
ONE	Which I won't feel.
TWO	Push my head back;
	In in one.
	There. Done.

TWO wipes off his hands –

ONE	He asked if I had any questions, and I said yes, just the one. When it actually happens, will it feel fast, or slow?

And pulls on a tatty wrapper or kimono. A silence.

TWO	And now what? Wait? Who *waits*, when they're twenty-one?
ONE	A new country, in a darkened room.
TWO	*I* could write to *him*, I suppose –
ONE	– and there was me thinking all that had ended.
TWO	In violet ink….
ONE	Ended four years ago. Or was it three….
TWO	….Or get dressed, find a cab, go into town anyway and get myself properly screwed for a change; exhibit myself at major railway stations –
ONE	*(As if he had heard him.)* Yes.
TWO	Start talk that there is competition for my love – use the word so loudly even he'll have to hear it. Meet some total stranger and promise to behave myself before he even asks. Promise not to ask who else he kisses, for instance. Promise not to laugh when he

leans into my face half way across Leicester Square and says excuse me but what do *You, Mean?* Promise not to say well it all depends who's asking – my mother never minds, but you, you look terrified you might wake up tomorrow morning to find I'd somehow slipped right inside you. Promise not to point out that making things mean something isn't my responsibility, actually, especially not on my birthday. Promise Everybody, Everything, All The Time.

Promise not to start a scene.

With a policeman.

ONE   For instance.

ONE laughs, which hurts.

TWO   Promise not to say out loud well why don't you hit me if you feel that strongly about it.

ONE   Ah yes.

TWO   Because I *love* the sound of tearing silk, actually.

Never to say–

ONE+TWO   Come on, hit me –

TWO   Hit me however and whenever you like–

ONE   I remember.

TWO   Because you're the solution to my problems, you are. You're the answer to all my questions. Better than brandy –

ONE   Exclamation!

TWO   – better than champagne from the bottle –

ONE   Quite –

TWO	You bring the blood right up to the surface, you do –
ONE	All over my fucking face –
TWO	That's right, and while we're indulging in the odd bit of public slap and bone-breaking, can I tell you a secret; can I tell you a secret, Officer?
ONE	Oh, the relief!

A fit of coughing.

TWO	This is a relief, actually; a relief. Now that you're finally here with your fucking hand on my fucking shoulder and I'm being arrested and it's all actually finally fucking happening, Officer, it's funny – funny that the one night I really need my *lover*, he just isn't here; he isn't here, and it looks like I'll have to get battered and booked all on my own. Bruises and silk, such a fetching combination – and when he sees it in the papers, I wonder if he'll ask himself, out loud for preference, oh, what I have I lost?
ONE	***(Taking another drink; hoarsely.)***
	No – no, I never collapsed. Not even when there was blood in my shoes.
TWO	No, Officer –
ONE	Quite –
TWO	No. Do I look as though I'm shaking? I've been practising, you see; practising *being myself* when I walk down the street. It rather suits me, don't you think? Fits me – fits me like a well-built gown. Well Mama does always say that the only things worth asking

45

for are the things for which it is far too much to ask. And it is, after all, my birthday –

SUDDEN KNOCKING. THREE KNOCKS. THINGS BECOME UNREAL.

TWO	Yes? What?
ONE	He promised.
TWO	No Mama!!! –
ONE	Ethyl Chloride.
TWO	Really.
ONE	Chloral Hydrate.
TWO	Yes, I will.
ONE	Diacetylmorphine.
TWO	I said I will!
ONE	He promised.
TWO	No, I'm sure nothing's wrong.
ONE	Promised me the ocean floor.
TWO	Nothing – he's just been delayed.
ONE	Oh just one question, I said.
TWO	Yes I know!
ONE	Just the one.
TWO	– I know that's the time.
ONE	Will it be quick, I said, or slow –
TWO	Twenty to fucking seven – as if it matters –

TWO *turns upstage in vexation. The sound of a young man's tears.*

ONE   When it comes. You can tell me. Come
on, don't be shy – you'll hardly be the first
man to see me stripped to the skin. Oh yes
Doctor – many. The first? The first man to
ever touch me? Let me see… I'll leave out
the ones who's names never mattered, shall
I? Time is short, after all. Let me…see.

A silence.

Louis – Louis was the first. He was also the
first to use the actual word to me. Out loud.
Afterwards.

Then Albert.

Alex, Gerard – and then I suppose Arthur.
For nearly two whole years. Two whole
years of silk and laughter, from our very first
meeting right up until

Right up until I received that January letter.

Arthur, and then, after some time, after I
had…recovered, Pierre.

Jack. Who was very skilled

Samuel. Who was very rich.

Edgar, who worked backstage.

Eugene…. I think.

Harry.

Sidney.

Reg.

Jim.

Walter.

And then, Arnold. I remember now. A man called Arnold, three years ago almost exactly – it wasn't love, but his were the last hands to ever touch me.

You think you can't end, but you do.

You think; you can't end. But you do.

You think you can't end. But, you do.

You know –

It never does mean that, does it?

She adds a drop more morphine to her glass. Then, unscrewing the top, she adds the whole of the rest of the bottle, emptying it. She looks at the now-fatal glass.

TWO turns.

O leave me alone why don't you. Leave me alone, in your room with no furniture. I'll be fine.

A silence. The glass.

That word. *Catastrophe.* Cat, Ah – Ah, exclamation mark – Cat, Ah, Strow, Fay – from the Greek…People use it all the time, don't they, and always so lightly? Catastrophe; the finale, upshot, finish or fuck-up; the thing from which there can be no recovery.

The Descending Hand, for instance.

The Smash; The Verdict.

The Razor, in a Darkened Hotel Room.

A letter in January.

A Diagnosis....

The thing from which there can be no return;

The Unsurviveable.

The kind of thing people like me got paid to play eight times a week.....eight times a week, for thirty fucking years –

A silence.

It took me a year to get rid of them – my dresses. A whole year. Some I scissored; some I gave away – but only to people chosen because I knew they could never understand one iota of what such a gift might mean. Some were abandoned under beds even I was ashamed of having climbed into. Some I burnt – then bent and broke what was left in the grate till it could be carried out wrapped in brown paper and left in some gutter like... Like an aborted child. Silk goes up easily, but you'd be surprised how much bone and metal there is in something that lies as well as a properly constructed dinner-gown...how much there is underneath.

Perhaps that was what I wanted – to find out what was underneath. What it is that... survives.

A whole year – a year, to make sure there was no possibility of my ever going back.

And then

I mean now. Now

She indicates the suit she is wearing. She touches it. Rage.

Now, I have no idea. No idea at all…

Not even how to say my name when they
ask me…

Oh!! People always used to ask when does it
start, the Change, The Transformation, when
does it start, but you know the real question
is when does it end; when do you finally
become The Other One…the one you were
never meant or allowed to be… the one you
Dreamt Of Being…and d'you know, I always
lied. I used to say Oh it's the hair –when the
hair goes up, that's definitely when I feel it,
it's simple really – or the shoes, – because
you see what people don't realise is that they
alter the whole way you walk, d'you see –
your ribs all line up differently, just here, do
you see? Or my lips – or the rings – hands,
so hard to disguise, don't you find, I always
leave putting them on till last, silly really
but. Or when I hear the music. Or when the
lights hit me, hard. You see what you have
to understand – I used to say, always, lying
–What you have to understand is that it's not
inside me, the Change, the Transformation;
it's my Job. Otherwise I'd go mad. D'you
see? I couldn't possibly be one person when
you look at and another when I look at
myself, because that would be impossible.
One on the outside and another on the
inside. D'you see? Impossible. One actual,
another imagined entirely. One sitting here,
and another when I'm on my back. One
when I wake, and one when I dream.

I mean, you'd go mad.

And I lied, because it doesn't end, ever. If
you're sitting there waiting for me to tell you

about the day the changing ends, the day that you *know* – if you're waiting for that then take it from me you're going to go home hungry and tired.

You choose, you change, you adjust, you enter, you take your place, but you never *know,* ever. You *decide.* Always. Every morning.

I am talking to all of you, by the way. Out loud. Under the circumstances. Never Knowing, but Always Deciding – Mama was right about that if nothing else. Never, and Always. That's the trick. Every night is the same night, and every morning is the only one that matters. Especially this one. Never, and Always. Thank you, and goodnight.

To an imaginary conductor in an imaginary pit;

Thank you –

She sings the number that always ended her act.

LIGHT ON THE OCEAN –

LIGHT ON THE HILL;

LIGHT OF DEVOTION,

GUIDING US STILL.

CALM IS THE EVENING,

BRIGHT WAS THE DAY –

NOW IT IS LEAVING

FADING AWAY…

LIGHT IT MUST LEAVE US

LIGHT IT MUST PART –

THAT SHOULD NOT GRIEVE US

HERE IN OUR HEARTS;

CALM IS THE EVENING

BRIGHT WAS THE DAY –

NOW IT IS LEAVING

FADING AWAY.

GONE ARE LIFE'S TREASURES,

HUSH'D IS ITS NOISE;

ENDED ALL PLEASURES,

ENDED ALL JOYS…

CALM IS THE EVENING,

BRIGHT WAS THE DAY

NOW IT IS LEAVING

FADING AWAY…

NOW IT IS LEAVING –

FADING AWAY!!

The ghost of applause.

The ghost of laughter.

Closed eyes.

TWO   *(Softly; young)*

Here's another one, one I've never told
anybody. It's my favourite of all my dreams.

I'm naked. I walk down the stairs, and out the front door with the air touching me all over. All of my soft places are exposed for once – unlocked. There's no bone, no metal, and not even any silk. Nobody on the bus says anything – they daren't. The air is quite hot, like kisses, and when I get there it… What's the word? Churns. Parts, to admit me. The pavements are packed as tight as a tin of pilchards, but nobody touches me – nobody says anything, not the whole night. Not a word, except; How lovely she is. What truly remarkable hair.

Sometimes I think it would work even better if everybody else in my dream was naked too. Imagine.

A silence.

Please. Somebody help me.

A silence.

ONE   **(*His eyes still closed.*)** I can't.

A silence.

TWO   Oh honestly, listen to yourself…..

ONE   I can't help you

TWO   Later. Later, he said.

And there was me thinking I was good at waiting…Alright;

Listen to yourself;

(A pantomime;)

It's ten to seven, there is nobody else here, but if there was; if *he* was; if Arthur was here, you'd say….

(A check in the mirror)

You'd say Well, since you've finally
appeared, what is it you have to tell me?
Come on.

ONE   I can't tell you anything.

TWO   I was expecting a letter, but since you've
come in person ….

I'm listening –

ONE   I can't– I can't *explain*, nobody can, you have
to live your own–

TWO   Oh yes you bloody can! Well?

A silence.

ONE   What is it you want to hear.

TWO   Almost anything you might have to say,
quite frankly.

ONE   Alright.

Try not to shock him. Downstairs, I mean.
Invent some clumsinesses of your own, so he
won't guess how much you know. Men never
like that.

TWO   And?

ONE   Try not to mind when he…when he leaves
you.

TWO   And?

ONE   Give me time! I have to think what matters
most.

Remember –

TWO   Remember what?

ONE	Remember that there will be others. And remember the moments when no one is watching you. I think they're all we really have.
TWO	For instance?
ONE	For instance, later tonight.
TWO	Are you alright?
ONE	Yes!!! Yes.
TWO	Please don't touch me.
ONE	I can't!!

A silence.

TWO	Sorry…
ONE	He *will* write. He will write, later, just like he said he would.
TWO	Go on.
ONE	And the boy who delivers his letter will be beautiful, in a uniform the colour of the ocean. You'll dress, and he'll arrive – in the cab, at last – and Mama will be delighted, noisily, and a fool. You'll disregard her, and climb in. On the journey, your silk will get crumpled – but not much; you'll mostly use it to keep him at a distance.
TWO	Of course.
ONE	There will be a ring – he'll give it to you in the cab. The box, after he's placed the ring on your finger, will snap shut as if it personally disapproved. You'll both laugh.
TWO	Will we – you know, I –
ONE	No! You never know! You never know.

TWO	Well excuse me.
ONE	Thank you. He'll use the word. Then, when you get there, the room will indeed be full, and the cerise silk much admired; there will be applause, and laughter, but first
TWO	Yes?
ONE	As he hands you down, his heel will catch your lace, and the noise it makes when it tears will be the exact sound of a woman screaming in another room, and you'll wonder if that's why we always wear it –
TWO	Oh listen to yourself.
ONE	and you'll want to turn and run, suddenly, but you won't. For which I admire you very much young man –
TWO	Honestly.
ONE	And after the ball is over – after the break of dawn – in that apartment which he rents so that nobody can hear you making all that noise, he'll do something they very rarely do. He'll look at you – look at you, while he's still inside you. No listen –

The light will be not unlike how it is now, just catching at the edges of things....

And showing you, yourself.

Yourself, reflected in his eyes. Naked. Entire. And worth loving.

He'll turn away of course, as they always do, but it'll be too late – you'll have seen yourself in the only mirror that ever matters.

The one you can never break.

The one you'll have to live with for years.

The one…… that shows you what you want.
It'll be –

TWO	Yes I know. I know.
ONE	A catastrophe.
TWO	Yes.
ONE	Catastrophe, exclamation.
TWO	Yes.
ONE	Always.

A long silence.

ONE	Thank you for listening to me. I must go – Oh – one thing – in the hospital, this morning, those will in fact be the last hands to ever touch me, won't they?
TWO	Sorry?
ONE	Won't they.
TWO	Yes.
ONE	So there are no new feelings after all.
TWO	No. Not any that matter, anyway.
ONE	Thank you. One more thing.
TWO	What?
ONE	It makes no sense to be frightened you might not die as yourself.
TWO	Why?
ONE	Because you can't really die as anybody else.

A silence.

Now do put some clothes on.

TWO   What?

ONE   You don't want him to find you unfinished,
       do you?

TWO hesitates – then –

TWO   No –

He begins hurriedly slapping on a face.

ONE   No…

TWO   *(Under his breath.)* Item, two lips.

ONE   Exactly. But you do have to hurry now I'm
       afraid –

TWO   Two true blue eyes….

ONE   Yes. Never mind fussing with the eyebrows –

TWO   One face.

ONE   Not *entirely* true – please hurry –

TWO   Just…the One…Face –

ONE   Oh christ…

*(ONE takes a dangerously deep swig of morphine to get him
through the last few moments before the knock on the door
comes)*

TWO   One face; mine….There!!

ONE   Yes! That's right, so that when he comes,you
       can say;

*(They both pantomime hearing a knock on the door, and
speak together)*

ONE +TWO   **Just a minute!**

ONE   Yes. And then…then, you say;

TWO	Actually I'm still not quite ready –
ONE	No!!! You say I'm ready! You say I'm fine with there being a mirror in the changing room, in fact I'm used to it. You say yes, I'll leave my clothes on the chair –
TWO	And then he comes in anyway– which is charming – And you say

A silence. ONE *stands. He speaks as if he was naked at the hospital.*

ONE	There. This is me.

A silence.

TWO	Well here you are at last.
ONE	Yes. At last.
TWO	Now, about those things for which it is too much to ask –
ONE	Yes?
TWO	About this *happiness* that I've heard mentioned so often.
ONE	Yes?
TWO	I want it. And I think sooner, rather than later.
ONE	Yes.
TWO	And we should talk about exactly how that's going to happen, don't you think?
ONE	Yes.
TWO	Now.
ONE	What?
TWO	I said *Now*

A silence.

ONE   Oh right.....Yes. Now. Thank you. Now.....
I'm ready.

A silence. ONE begins to leave. He halts, and looks back at TWO.

ONE   That's right. You hold out your hand, and
you say:

TWO holds out his hand.

TWO   Arthur....

A silence.

KNOCKING.

Darkness. The piece ends.